For Edmund

all good wishes

in our common

campaign for good

literature

Oxford

4 April 1967.

A.L.

Poems of
Cornwall and America

books by A. L. Rowse

*

Poetry

POEMS OF A DECADE

POEMS CHIEFLY CORNISH

POEMS OF DELIVERANCE

POEMS PARTLY AMERICAN

Prose

A CORNISH CHILDHOOD

A CORNISHMAN AT OXFORD

CORNISH STORIES

WILLIAM SHAKESPEARE: A BIOGRAPHY

SHAKESPEARE'S SONNETS
Edited with an Introduction and Notes

CHRISTOPHER MARLOWE: A BIOGRAPHY

SHAKESPEARE'S SOUTHAMPTON

THE ENGLISH SPIRIT

TIMES, PERSONS, PLACES

Poems of Cornwall and America

A. L. ROWSE

FABER AND FABER
24 Russell Square
London

First published in mcmlxvii
by Faber and Faber Limited
24 *Russell Square London WC*1
Printed in Great Britain
by the Bowering Press Plymouth

TO

CHARLES CAUSLEY

Sailor, Poet, Cornishman

PREFACE

HITHERTO my poetry has been anchored to, and reflected the environment of, Oxford and Cornwall. With this volume, my fifth, the emphasis shifts mainly to America; and I hope it may have this at least to recommend it, that very few English poets have written much of American landscapes and scenes. Here is the modern world.

Yet, arranging these poems for publication, I have been struck by the continuity of themes with earlier volumes, consistency of mood and attitude through the years, even a return in later life to the earliest such as one might not have expected. (So many of my contemporaries have ceased to write verse. The age is certainly unpropitious to poetry).

In a climate in which poetry is hard put to it to exist, in a time when little inspires or even encourages, perhaps there is something to be said for a poetry that is unrhetorical and realist, keeping its authenticity by keeping to the ground, and so avoiding the overemphatic, the pretentious and untrue, the just plain bogus—the bane of so much contemporary art.

A lifetime is a life, not the less authentic for being consistent with itself at different periods: in the secrecy of poetry it is possible to write one's innermost autobiography, as Hardy found.

A. L. ROWSE

CONTENTS

II

I

Setting Sail in the Fall of 1961

Southampton sways with the great ship turning,
The cranes approach, the derricks dip and bob:
The world swings round on its axis
Into a wilderness of water.
Everything swims into a different focus:
The liners were head-on, now present their sides,
Red and black funnels, lavender-white flanks;
Gatcombe, *Romsey*, *and Clausentium*
Heave and tug, plough up the waters,
Warp and weave, chug and smoke,
Draw near each other, strain at the hawser,
Till the immense vessel slews round:
The crowded terminal a coloured parterre
Where people stand still with surprise,
Silent and hushed as the ritual of the sea unfolds,
Having said their separate goodbyes,
A few wave handkerchiefs hopeless of identification:
No-one moves, the terminal itself swings into position,
Passengers lined up on an ultimate deck.
O, which is ship and which is terminal,
Which are those on land and those at sea,
All alike under the destiny
Naufragantis saeculi?

In Mid-Atlantic

Bergs of clouds and mountains of surf,
Five seagulls follow the great ship
In mid-Atlantic, where the rainbows
Haunt the horizon,
A column of colour joining cloud and sea,
Lighting up a fancied landscape toward
Greenland and Labrador;
Or reflected in another sector of sky,
Moses' pillar of fire reigning over
Ahab's world of waters.
Turn to the south, the silver track of sun
That leads to the Azores and fabled
Atlantic islands sought for with longing
By Henry, Prince and Navigator,
Virgin and seer, whose eyes
Sought some certain end not known to men
Under those skies.

Pilgrimage to America

That I all unbelieving should have to be the priest
Saying the last prayers by her bedside
How strange a fate, like everything
In the involuntary mesh in which caught
I had my experience of life,
Unknowing, unknown, all unforewarned,
Yet with strange intimations of the truth
Occasionally glimpsed through the veil
Of make-believe I held for truth:
The face at the window saying farewell
To the child apart that might be his,
The sense of the man whose track I follow
Across the Atlantic, whose image haunts me
On these pilgrimages without purpose
(Or is the purpose also withheld from me,
This the unknown reason why I go?)
Of a man long dead, under his mound now
In Montana, his warfare accomplished,
Leaving never a word, a signal, a gesture,
To one following in his footsteps
To say he ever knew, or was aware.
In myself I recognise some of his traits,
Temerarious like him, like him impatient,
Cursing the fate that is in oneself,
But most of all the temperament of the gambler
Whose ideas were too big for his boots,
Leading him to cross the Atlantic,
To find a wider scope and at length a grave
By the foothills in far-off Montana.

On the Dead President

I will not perturbate
Thy paradisal state
With praise
Of thy dead days.
Francis Thompson

How like the age to lop the tallest flower,
An age that envies difference, quality.
On this malign day the mountains are lovelier still:
The San Gabriel range looks down unknowing
Upon the old fractured Mission of his faith,
Where the fathers lived their spartan lives
Among the Indians, *Cordis Mariae Filii.*
Levavi oculos meos in montes,
unde venit auxilium mihi.
Today the scene is sadder for its unfeeling beauty,
Unconcerned with the ills of man, unsharing
Our suffering and grief for loss irreparable.
The cool and golden head that held all clear
Shattered by an irrelevant lunatic shot;
The voice that spoke hope to a discordant world
Suddenly stilled, in the twinkling of an eye,
In the evil glint from an upper window;
The courage that had come through the waters of the Pacific,
The plaudits and the abuse of the mob alike,
Stopped by a bullet in a chance Texan street:
Everything in that too fortunate life—
The golden youth so carefully groomed,
So nurtured, so prepared for politics,
The clarity of mind, the boyish grin—
All fated to lead to this unmeaning moment.
This meeting with destiny, this encounter,
From what different paths, of the slayer and the slain.
The map of life, full of promise and smiling hope,
All spread out like a mountain slope

With many honeyed folds and tawny flanks,
Suddenly crumpled in a blood-stained car.
To what purpose? To what end?
Nothing that can portend
Any good to the human condition;
Nothing that means anything,
Or speaks anything but misery for all.
Let him that can, then, pray—for what
Consolation that offers in a faithless time,
When even crime has no gesture of grandeur,
Nothing in it but what is significant and mean
To bring disgrace upon the human scene:
Deus auxilium meum et spes mea in Deo est.
Deus, adjutor noster in aeternum.

An Episode in the Korean War

See these three G.I.'s caught in the eye of a camera:
There has been some accident of war, or all too usual event.
One of them reads gravely from a book,
A service-book, the service of the dead.
The youngest one, the little fellow, in hysteria
Has thrown himself into the arms of his mate,
Who holds close to him the small head,
Neat fist clenched in grief
For his buddy dead.
The large, long-fingered hands enfold,
Spread-eagle the tensed-up back,
Console the shaken, childish frame.
The noble head looks gravely down,
Inclining gently towards the grieving boy,
Grief graven too in the grown man's look.
The third goes on reading from the book:
Greater love hath no man than this, that
    a man lay down his life for his friends.
The grave in the foreground is unseen.

Popham's Beach

(for Rick Harwell)

September sea-mist swathes the long fingers into the ocean:
This is the land of Kennebec, Penobscot and Pemaquid.
Quiet inland waters stand reflective among the reeds.
Follow the road among rocks and early cemeteries,
The lobster-men's cabins, fringed by fall-asters and golden
rod,
Past the silent bittern camouflaged beside the road.
The Ojibways call him He-looks-at-the-sun,
And so he does, long neck tilted up to eye the man.
Brave by the road a pheasant, old redcoat, stands sentinel;
In the creek a heron plunges beak into the sludge.
Red of sumach, gold of yellow birch,
A sparrow-hawk crosses the lemon reeds,
The chipmunks, striped gold, run the roads;
Through the pinebelt, and we are arrived at the sea:
After the woods and rocks the sweet rank scent
Of seaweed piling up the wrack of the past,
A half-moon of sand, islands out to sea,
A world of singing surf in the ears,
The combers breaking upon the sandbars,
As when they built their fort between river and ocean,
And first wintered in the New World of America:
Honest old George Popham, of an unwieldy body
And timorously fearful to offend;
Ralegh Gilbert with all the arrogance of his family,
A loose life, prompt to sensuality,
Humorous, headstrong, of small judgment and experience.
The preacher was most to be commended
Both for his pains in his place and his honest endeavours.
Here along edge of the sea we tread in their tracks.
The store-house burned over their heads,

The agèd President died in the bitter winter,
While they worked upon the pinnace *Virginia*,
And all elected to return home in the spring.

In Central Park

The bones of original America show through the grass.
Autumn is in the acacias turning, the planetrees sloughing their skin, and in the hips and haws.
September warmth has brought out the exiles, the hopeless of heart stretched along the benches.
A sick bird looks up for pity, where pity is improbable.
Fat blondes jabber in German, ease off their shoes, ankles swollen over.
Here in this place where Columbus confronts Shakespeare,
And FitzGreene Halleck—a poet of whom one does not hear—
Confronts nobody, looks up in portentous inspiration,
One of the people for whom this show is meant
Has put a cigarette box in the hand of the bard.
Who cares?
The pigeons ruffle and preen in muddy pools;
An unpopular grackle forages for himself with plaintive cries.
A Chinese negro passes, strange pride of race in such a face.
Nurses push dribbling children in fringed perambulators
Along the paths, these asphalt glades
Where a tamed Diana still affects to hunt the woods,
Arrested in stone,
Like this civilisation without a soul,
In search of one.

The Six o'Clock from Grand Central

Six o'clock, Grand Central, Track Thirty Four,
The Twentieth Century Limited awaits
Tired business executives after a rugged day
From R.C.A., Rockefeller Center, 666 Fifth Avenue,
And many another office-building in Manhattan.
With weary step and slow they descend the ramp,
Step into room, roomette, allotted space
In coaches that already open up
Vistas of a now submissive continent,
The Mystic, Merrimack and Mistanee.
The train moves slowly through the suburbs of the city
And out along the winking verge of the Hudson,
Lists like a ship around the curve of the river,
The jade-lighted bridges that span the void,
Up the incline to Harmon, Albany, Syracuse,
On through a night punctuated with lights
To Toledo, Elkhart, Englewood, Chicago.

Independence Square

The half moon of late November
Looks down on Independence Square.
The slums are cleared, the gardens rise,
The fountains play to the unheeding people
More intent on the Army and Navy Game.
Myrmidons of Army and Navy parade
The streets in groups, or with their girls.
The trees are yet young, younger than they:
Crategus and maple, cherry and crouched juniper,
Leafless sumach, bunched berries at end of bough;
The lampstands are erect, and shaded lights
Squat like toadstools upon the matted ivy.
Buses coagulate upon the streets
To Chestnut and Spruce, Walnut Street and Vine.
Have a Pepsi! Save at Fidelity!
New Size, Your Size, '61 *Chevy.*
The neon lights blink, blot out the moon:
Independence is diminished, lost
Amid the monoliths of modern America.

The Golden God

Autumn flies in all the flags
And in the melancholy sound of many waters.
Juniper fringes the vacant space where soon
The variegated figures will dance their ballet,
Cut their capers on the frozen parquet
Under the high and leering moon.
Now on a September Sunday afternoon
The clouds billow above the monoliths of stone,
Sun comes and goes on the glass menageries
And on the golden water-god arrested in mid-motion,
Curtained by falling spray in the act of blessing
His parterres of restricted ocean.
The polyglot crowds pass and repass,
Express surprise and pleasure in their rapid tongues,
Extrapolation of an older continent.
The innocent, spectacled sailors of the new
Look for objects for their affections,
For some affiliation to their land,
For security
After the sea,
For the tomb
Of the sought womb.

Pavements

The pathos of people on the pavements
Hoping to attract amorous attention:
Each woman views herself in the window,
This one in violet to emphasize the eyes,
That one in mink to show that she is rich.
Another, with green scarf bound around the brow,
Tiptoes crazily along on stiletto heels.
One with head carefully arranged as bird's nest,
The next, a negress, has removed the natural curl
To give the sinister Chinese effect;
Above a plain face, hair coiled like a snake
Ready to strike at the unnoticing passer-by.
In every eye insatisfaction, longing to attain
Something for ever unattainable,
Always around the corner of the possible,
Always on the alert for something to turn up,
When, if it does, it but staves off despair
Briefly, for a moment, without even the aid
Of illusion any more, vacuity returns,
The avid stare in a thousand eyes
Reflected in windows with the wintry skies.

Married Couple

They have nothing to say to each other,
Having said it all a hundred times before.
Now they sit face to face in the hotel dining-room,
He slightly askew, apologetic, a quiet bore,
Spectacled, lean hands spread in deprecating
Gesture, as a hundred times before.
She sits, tiny, coiled, an electric spring,
Clad all in black, false pearls at fat neck,
Very well made up, girl's hair parted in the middle
Falling short on the nape, still nut-brown,
Middle age revealed only in the creased skin,
Short of sight, the perceptible second chin,
The restless eyes blinking crossly at her spouse,
Small feet out of her shoes dancing with disdain.
The placid breadwinner settles to his steak;
She fidgets with the crabmeat on her plate,
The dietetic grapefruit, slimming fare.
They have nothing to say.
Then the baby-face leans forward, stabs the air
With slim forefinger, wrinkled hands betray
Middle age, eyes cross with lassitude,
Sparkling with contempt, the brilliants on her ring
Mocking the gold and quiet band
On his hand, badge of his servitude.

The Species

The natural instinct of the male for the female
Is something universal, hardly comprehensible.
The fat Jew taximan on the way to Idlewild
Notices the nondescript nurse at the corner of the block.
'You like them dark?'
'Yeah, I prefer them dark—more aggressive.'
The cab half-slews. 'Want a taxi, miss?'
A smile is exchanged. At the airport
The tall New Englander in navy blue,
Unsmiling Puritan appearance, automatically
Appraises the barely decipherable girl going by.
I have known in an ancient common-room
A young stallion snort at female voices in the quad.
What is it to be shut out from this play of life?
One observes, with Henry James, the human aquarium:
All the fish going round, sad jaws working,
Eyes bulging in ever-unsatisfied stare,
Enclosed within their element, scale on scale,
        Quite unaware
That the female of the species is more deadly than the male.

Last Things

Look thy last on all things lovely
Every hour
Walter de la Mare

Certainly look thy last on all things every hour,
For who knows what, at any minute, may turn up?
Behold the city spread below you, block on block,
Inspiring spectacle from the plane that last week
Plunged into Boston harbour with large loss of life.
Or there's the train that, crossing the viaduct,
Inexplicably leaps the parapet.
The Atlantic liner while still only off New York
Is holed in collision and founders in a fog.
The car, swiftly swerving to avoid a dog,
Eliminates a loftier life than his.
Fear the stranger in the hotel bedroom who
Threatens to throw himself from the window
But, thinking better of it, performs the act on you.
What if the surly, sullen negro should
Feel himself insulted and turn round
Upon the admirer of such strength and grace,
Smash his face, deliver a blow
From which there is no recovery?
Or the *matelot* in the *bas-fonds* of Marseilles,
The matador of the *Ponce de Leon* in Madrid?
Such meditations still trouble the midnight
And the noon's repose. No remedy but to
Look thy last on all things every hour.

Riches

The riches of my later life offset
Many frustrations and resentments earlier:
Long illness, straightened circumstance,
Hardly a day outside the parish bounds,
Walking the road wherever I went,
Proud, humiliated, but yet unbent,
No scope, nor variety, rooted in depth
And narrow intensity. Now I am content
Within a hotel bedroom in a foreign land,
My familiar possessions on either hand,
The old clothes-brush known since childhood,
My faithful slippers accompanying me
Into unfamiliar, unknown territory,
Mettatuxet, Winnepesaukee, Narragansett Bay,
Where the solar geese in V-formation
Fly into the sunset and south for Louisiana.
My window looks out not on *The Boston Evening Transcript*
But on *The Providence Journal*, *The Evening Bulletin*,
On *Downtown's Most Centrally Located Parking Station.*
The honeyed light of late Indian summer
Spills through the lattices of the American blind,
The Venetian blind of childhood at Tregonissey—
How remote in time and mood rather than memory,
For I remain still faithful to continuity,
The garnered heaps of grain stored in my granary,
Richly glowing to feed on with thanksgiving,
Plunge my hand in the golden dust,
Stirring up motes in the sun
As in those harvests far away,
To console in days to come and not dismay.

Muskingum

'Jesus increased in wisdom and stature, and in favour with God and man.'

Away from the Presbyterian platitudes of the college
Here is a place where the chipmunks forage
Gold-striped in the grass, sit up to eye
The suspect stranger.

Mid-morning, yet the Hallow-e'en moon
Leers high over the girls' gaunt dormitory,
Where they dream their innocent dreams to be
Mothers of the nation.

Sycamores, maples, willows, dogwood—
A blue jay scolds the quiet neighbourhood;
The monogamous swans in conjugal amity
Patrol the lake.

Blue asters fringe the stream below the Fall
Tapestry of verdure, russet and gold.
A sanctus bell breaks the silence to recall
The ages of faith.

Penetrate the Hollows, where the leaves
Have lived their lives and now detach themselves
Softly from the trees, with papery sound
Fall to the ground.

The fallen giant of primeval forest gives
The illusion of Châteaubriand's Ohio:
At the end of the sunlit glade Atala
Perhaps may appear.

Over the rustic bridge the pretty girls pass,
Rackets in hand. The leaves strew the grass
Even as they will be strewn in their season:
Since all things pass.

Under the Pillared Portico

Driven by the mad professor in the beaver hat
Into the campus superfluously late at night,
Up the snow-covered, ice-bound hill
Suddenly, swiftly swerving round the bend
I catch sight of a lighted scene to chill
The heart, a blow between the unwilling eyes:
Under the arclight of the pillared portico
A rite enacted on the open stage,
Oblivious of time and light and passers-by.
There in the eye of the world for all to see,
Uncaring, mute, in silent ecstasy,
Two lovers in passionate stillness: he
Tall and columnar, slender as the pillar
Erect before the sacrificial act,
Gold-crowned as the god; while she
Held in his arms in one unconscious world
With him. 'Each hath one and is one'
Might be their motto, if they had heard of Donne,
'John Donne, Undone'—by love undone;
Nor any more aware than he
What time will do to turn the trance to prison,
Reveal no world to discover
In one or other lover.
Such are the thoughts that rage
In that age of unwanted revelation
While the car wheels round
And with it the darkened city.

Saturday Afternoon in Madison, Wisconsin

The Saturday afternoon dog barks his head off
On the deserted porch. Improbably
A cockerel crows in the grounds of the campus.
Mount the slope amid the animals
Sculpted in ice, monuments in the snow:
Tortoise extended, squirrel with tail in air,
Couchant cat after a bird, a sad old man
With the hollow eyes of Montezuma
Or Ozymandias, king of kings.
The pretty sculptresses have departed
Home for the week-end to Winnebago,
Windsor or Fair Oaks, Monona or Waunakee.
Love overflows the expectant city
In this suspended moment hung in the air,
Awaiting spring in the rose-tipped elms,
In the powdered flush on the virgin lake.
Enter the hall, tiptoe along the corridors
Where the water-fountains make music
To themselves, no-one to hear.
Look in at the deserted class-rooms:
Here is one I occupy for a fragment of time
And then pass by, not even a memory
To students themselves become ghosts,
Who come and go
Like motes uncounted in the sun:
Even we,
Even so.

Evening Walk in the Middle West

Go down Dayton Street and up Hamilton Avenue
To Jefferson Square, where a few
Lights linger in the Capitol, though
The legislators have departed.
A mob of English sparrows cling
To the inclement ledges of Woldenbergs.
Have a coke with your pizza, chicken, shrimp,
Your spaghetti, spareribs, sandwiches.
Across the dormitory houses the banners hang:
Season in the Sun—Judy.
It's elementary—Watson.
Presenting Polly. Now it's Bonnie.
The earnest chaste young faces pass by
Numb with innocence and naiveté.
The Lenten devotees spill out of the Catholic Church
That elbows St. Columba's Presbyterian Church
That nudges the First Methodist Church,
Mother of all the Methodist churches in Madison.
Across the street the pompous portico
Of the First Church of Christ Scientist proclaims:
Our Faith is in God, Our hope is in immortality,
Our Love is toward all mankind.
A civilisation built on bromide,
Kindness, colourlessness, triviality—
And underneath, the violence and the reality.

The Tree

The chestnut tree at the corner of Gorham Street
Holds up its candelabra to the unheeding crowd.
The young women sway their skirts for the men,
The men in jeans display their curves to the girls,
In this draughty Mid-Western capital
Where the Capitol's gilt image of Liberty
Nods to Old Glory on high at the University.
The sad and splendid tree is humiliated between
Leon's Beauty Salon and Bendheim's Underwear,
Looks across at the immense and luminous
SHELL sign for ever gyrating on axis:
'Shell's On Top', 'Cars *Love* Shell':
The usual squalid city spectacle.
Aloft, aloof and very lonely
Amid neon lights and night-signs
The solitary tree recalls
Improbable memories of Tractarian Oxford,
Of Newman and Manning and the heresy
Of unregenerate baptism.
Here in this land of the living dead,
This spiritual waste:
No dynasties beneath the grass,
Only the wraiths of vanished Indians,
Winnebagoes or Menominees,
Fishing in their filth and squalor
Beside their four remembered lakes.

The Arboretum

(for Madeleine Doran)

She showed me Canada violets, white
With yellow centres, the petals blue
On the underside; delicate lavender waterleaf
In small blue clusters; wild woodland phlox
At foot of trees eloquent in the glades;
Everywhere underfoot ground-ivy or mint,
Blue with diminutive skullcaps along the stalk.
Here is a clearing in the burr-oak copse
Made for crab-apple, blossom blown over now,
But cherry's still white along the bough:
An amphitheatre in this far Forest of Arden
Made for *As You Like It* or the *Dream.*
Here by the stream we pause where migrant birds
Splash and make play on their way north in spring.
Down into the wood we plunge, and stay
To hear woodthrush and meadowlark answer his mate,
The catbird delighting the others to imitate.
Here underfoot is a long Indian mound
That in its shape counterfeits animal or bird.
No sound between us is uttered, no word.
Suddenly a blob of crested crimson is there:
The cardinal seeking food for his mate in the nest.
In the marsh below each redwinged blackbird,
A doctor of divinity in scarlet and black,
Clings to his separate pulpit, the bulrush swaying.
Across the lake tall cottonwoods are waving,
The shimmering popples turn silver in the wind.
We descend through what has become primeval
Forest in the mind, bridal-wreath in spray,
To the spring where, flung beneath a tree,
Two lovers unheeding are hot in bird-play,
She, beneath, pretending to resist,

He with all his length on top of her.
Alert, unnoticing, we make our way
To the water's edge. If this were England now
There would be church-bells in the late afternoon,
Ringing to church across the still lagoon.

Farewell to Wisconsin

Through the open door at end of corridor
Abraham Lincoln presides from his chair
Over the view down Bascom hill, up State Street
To the Capitol, now nudged by outsize buildings.
To the left, the lake at length unfrozen runs blue,
The lawns are trenched and hoed and weeded
Yet furnish their quota still of waste paper and milk
containers.
In the path a cadet holds hands with his girl.
Behind, the carpeted bluff marked with stone
In memory of some bluff Norwegian
Professor or Dean, looks over the furrowed plain
Of the lake marching east under the wind,
And at last it is spring.
Spring in the air, wine-like, beneficent,
Spring in the light, lemon and gold on bark of trees,
In the hoary heads of trees bursting into bloom
Under blue sky and puff-ball cloud
Sailing away and away across the Middle West.
This winter of my content is over,
Winter of escape, isolation, withdrawal,
Marooned like the figures in sculpted ice
On this alien slope in sun and snow:
A warmer winter world in which to inhabit
Than that become too familiar, too well known,
Where I have learned the art to spurn,
To which, reluctant, I return.

Arrival at L.A.

Oleander, palm, hibiscus, yucca,
Sepulveda Boulevard, the Security First National Bank,
To tell us we have arrived at Los Angeles.
Ahead the Verdugo hills, reminiscent of Tuscany,
Terra-cotta coloured and serrated ridge
Of old earthquake country.
Here begin eucalyptus, peppers, camphor trees,
The cuttings carpeted with purple lantana.
Now Inglewood Park cemetery, where lies
The dust of a small child of my blood and bone,
A child wise and sad beyond his years,
Who once looked long into my eyes,
Was frightened by what he saw,
Something beyond tears.
The airport-bus billows along Florence Avenue,
Past Realtors, Refrigerators, Records, Eat with Joe,
Every solicitation of eye and ear and taste.
Not a breath in the air. Sweat pours down behind the ears.
The scarecrow palms gesticulate
Above the desolation of houses. We journey
In gathering dusk towards still sun-tipped peaks.

San Juan Capistrano

(for Marcellus Steadman)

Twelve years have passed since I was here,
Filled with what alarms and toils, and one great grief.
Today, as before, the peppers planted by the friars
Wave their tresses over the adobe walls
That skirt the Camino Real, running its snake-like length
Two thousand miles from Mexico to Monterey.
The flag flies at half-mast for the dead President.
The November wind up the valley from the sea
Stirs in the trees, in the feathers of white doves
That croon about the walks, remembers the friars.
Nothing is further from the mind of the populace
Feeding the pigeons, photographing each other,
Bird on arm or head, bird-eye, bird-mind.
The blood-red blooms of hibiscus, golden
Bird-of-Paradise, flame-vine are out in flower.
Soft crooning fills the Californian afternoon.
Scarlet poinsettias, thirsty, drink the sun.
Within, the paraphernalia of the Faith,
Treasured possessions of the expatriate fathers,
Early vestments of the first Mexican missions,
A retablo from Barcelona, have come to rest
Here far from home. The scent of incense
Recalls one to the church: within is home.
Two Mexican couples, descendants of the faithful,
Swarthy youths with their bright-eyed, blue-silk girls,
Genuflect to the manner born. The hours pass.
Outside, the ancient mossy fountain is profiled
Against low, green hills, the splash of water falls
On into pale evening and into the placid nights
Filled with what nostalgia, with what passions
Suppressed, the regrets of men marooned for life
Between impassable mountains and trackless sea.

Here are the rosaries sculpted by the Indians,
A few shards of porcelain from far Majorca.
A carillon rings the hour to quivering arums,
The toyon berries are rich and ruddy as blood.
An English sparrow approaches, eyes the stranger,
Seems out of place under these exotic skies.
Here is the calaboose where refractory Indians
Were punished and confined behind the bars.
But where are the irons? Where the whips and thongs?
Something has changed in my life,
Turning all to iron, alike behind bars,
Something is wanting, expressible
In the one unspoken word.

San Marino

Bougainvillea spreads an exotic welcome
To the homekeeping traveller surprised
To find himself here: the library lost
In a garden of palms and Californian oaks
Along the geological fault that runs
From Santa Barbara south to San Diego.
From former rancho an English estate he flung
Around him like a cloak, with careful gesture
Manoeuvring the trees into their proper place,
Erecting a Palladian villa on its terrace,
Pivoted on the mountains, criss-crossed by alleys
Punctuated by marble goddesses, Juno
And Ceres blessing the fruits, while Mercury
Speeds with caduceus along the glades.
The palms strip their skin in the crackling heat,
The humming-birds, vibrant with delight,
Feed on the crimson of naked flowering coral.
Timid scholars take the place of the last tycoon,
Eat their frugal lunch beside the ponds
Where bluegills spawn beneath the lotuses;
Jays play bo-peep in the erythias,
Or flutter in the dry fringes of papyrus.

Here is cactus land, with jacaranda
And joshua-trees and flame of ocotillo:
Plants stand erect like columns in a temple,
Are tethered snakes upon the desert paths,
Or green flesh takes on the texture of jade,
An improbable flower upon tip of tongue;
The delicate fingers of the deodars,
The Spanish grace of olive-trees like dancers
Holding themselves ready for the dance,

Crêpe-myrtle thick as English hawthorn
In May, in which the treefrogs chirp all night.
The mounting foliage of magnolia
And avocado towering above the dust,
The heavy-sweet scent of the orange-trees
Comes and goes with the pulse of the fragrant heat,
Date-palms strew their yellow globes on the grass,
While persimmons glow like golden moons amid
The verdure of a Renaissance tapestry.
—O, all ye plants and fruits and seeds of the earth,
Praise ye the multi-millionaire who called
All this to life and now lies quiet enough
In the marble mausoleum, rising chaste,
Austere amid the aromatic groves
Between the San Gabriel mountains and the sea.

Et in Arcadia ego

Carob, locust and magnolia,
Eucalyptus and every kind of gum
Fringe the avenues to the Arboretum,
The people's paradise, fallen now from its high
Estate, when it was Lucky Baldwin's ranch.
When it was Lucky Baldwin's, one never knew
Whether the race-horses or the women
Stepped higher or proved the faster.
The Master regarded both with equal favour.
Here are the stables for thirty horses,
The barouche, dirty now, whence Lola Montez
One day dismounted to greet her familiar
Friends from the *demi-monde*.
Here is the portico which Lucky himself
Would come out upon of an evening
After a good dinner, gardenia or carnation
In cheerful buttonhole, no more deceived
By sycophants, the insolence of wealth,
Than by an upward turn of the wheel of fortune,
Knowing, like Apemantus observing Timon,
The downward would as certainly follow.

Now the more domesticated ducks
Paddle around the muddied pond,
More content, more philosophical,
Than their squandering precursors:
Whose duck's descendants have survived
Bankruptcy, divorce, desertion,
Tremblements de terre and all that's human,
Fatuous and mean. They cast
An understanding eye upon the scene,

Tolerant of all that passes, occasionally
Bat an eyelid in the sun; nor complain
Through the long hot Californian afternoons.

II

Passing By the Coast of Cornwall

After long exile and many leagues of water
Suddenly, framed in the port-hole, I see
A pictured lighthouse rise erect,
Nothing around it but the sea.
Then, hurrying on deck, I detect
Reefs and rocks and fragmentary isles,
Recognise it for the Bishop and know the land.
The coast of Cornwall comes into view
Very virginal and white in first sunlight;
Summer is over all the green pastures:
My heart beating against the ship's rail
Knows it for home.
See, the tower of St. Buryan church stands up,
The eastern face washed by morning sun;
Not far away I figure the Nine Maidens
Who, dancing on Sunday, were turned to stone.
There are the cliffs, the familiar places
Recognisable, recognised only by me
As the ship goes by and passengers crane to see
Land. 'What land is it?'—a foreigner turns to me
To ask. 'What land, indeed?'
Shall I deny him, as I was denied?
Pride refuses to utter the word:
'This is the coast of Cornwall.'
A bitter coast for those that know it well,
Full of the salt of the sea applied
To green wounds unstaunched, unhealed,
In spite of long silence and abstention.
See, I recognise the green field
By Ludgvan church tower, and Gulval;
Low down on the line is the Mount,
No guarded vision that looks towards Bayona's hold

But lying homely and snug at the end of the bay.
Mousehole, Newlyn, Penzance, Marazion:
There are the white houses along the shore
Caught in the sun. There are the towers
Of the churches. It needs only the scent of flowers
To be wafted, the bells to ring out
For the sea-folk to rise from their caves,
Approach once more the sunlit shore
Where a faithless mortal
Left lonely for ever
The kings of the sea.
The great ship leans to the land, then turns away;
My heart leans with the ship, then turns away.

The Little Land

(for Marthe Bibesco)

There is a taste upon the tongue
    if only I could recapture it
Of smouldering summer seas
    running in upon the coast
Or perhaps the sibilance of leaves
    frilled by the breeze from valley's mouth
In the mind such mixture of *wohlgemuth*
    images around the corner of the eye
Of the ferry-boat arriving at the quay
    nosing her way into Percuil
Riverside St. Mawes festive and gay
    with tousled summer visitors
Or visiting our toy cathedral town
    from the petunias of Treseder's in Cathedral Lane
    to Pellymounter's musty bookshop in Pydar
        Street.
How to savour the hours upon the palate
    the honeyed hours of the little land
    with their accumulated memories?
Here is the white gate to Trewithen
    so often passed by with my friend
Now open to me, the hidden pleasances,
    the shadowy park and all within
Panelled rooms of old Sir Christopher
    portraits of Hawkins and Zachary Mudge
    a kingdom of camellias beyond.
The garnered riches of my later life
    are everywhere I turn on every hand.
Here beneath the balcony of the Fowey Hotel
    Q. walks once more in the seaward garden
A more distant memory still
    I see myself a schoolboy

Panting up Polruan hill in the hot afternoon
to Lanteglos Polperro Looe
One Sunday trudging down the lane to Lansallos
the tower dark against the sunset sky
The bells suddenly burst out ringing
sweet and clear to evensong
Or looking down from the cliff upon
the cornered cove at Talland
Blue sea lapsing idly in
over seaweed and white sand
Presided over by the campanile built
upon the living rock looking out to sea
Or high on his inland perch
the hermit of Roche
Beckons from his roofless beacon
over the moor to Hensbarrow
North Goonbarrow, Lower Ninestones,
the corrugated ridge of Helman Tor
Dark in the distance lies
enchanted Luxulyan
Of long boyhood walks up the Valley
and round by the church
Where ivied traceries on cool
moorstone-mullioned windows
slaked the thirst of summer and youth
Raging in the mind matted
with wild convolvulus
Red Admirals feeding on pink
clumps of hempagrimony
Early lemon shoots of bracken
and tang of camomile
Filling every crevice of the heart
with remembered honey stored
To feed on with thanksgiving
in dark days to come.

The Road to Roche

(for Beatrice Peters)

Here is the hard-bitten country of my birth.
In a dank corner between monkey-puzzle and sawpit
Lived, drunken Dick Spargo: how he made a living
I've often wondered—occasionally cattle-dealing
And his wife's bit of property, I suppose.
Fridays he'd come rolling home from market,
His breeches as tight, and every variety
Of knobbly stick or cane or switch to brandish,
Long moustaches dripping booze at ends.
A grammar-schoolboy I mocked him with *Spargens*
Humida mella soporiferumque papaver.
On an island-site of its own, grim and gaunt
Like a flat-iron, the house of a double murder.
I knew the murderer: a stranger to the village,
Choirman and St. John's ambulance-man,
Sharp-nosed, evasive, sexy and saturnine.
The cottage gardens among granite crevices
Are not less bright with aubretia and saxifrage.
At the end of the garden-path the Vivians lived
To themselves behind their escallonia hedge:
A family of men, dark and voluptuous,
Who owned and worked their quarry in the moor,
Could ring the jumpers in more senses than one,
Like ringing the changes on a peal of bells,
Grandsire major or minor Stedman triple,
Experts in campanology and girls.
Here is Bethesda Chapel where Mamie and Frank
Sang their way into each other's favour
And further, clinching the matter up Look-out lane,
Amid flowering hawthorn and prickly furze,
Where all the girls got pregnant in the spring.
Careful! the car slews round the half-moon curve

To Carclaze timber-yard where father worked,
The jingling teams came home from Crinnis woods
With props for the pits; and still along the banks
Lie the great decapitated trunks—
One hears the cries of crashing and fallen trees.
See, here from the bourgeois verandah of butcher Trays
Breaks into view the sudden beauty of the bay,
Profile of Black Head, the shorn pines of Trenarren
Echo the pines of the Pincio, and shortly the Gribben
Pushes a long lizard paw into the sea.
Higher and higher, mount the last heave of hill
To where the china-clay country begins:
The pyramids rise pure in colour and line,
On the other hand, the chasms torn in the earth
Vertiginously deep and frightening.
By the wayside pool my old great-uncle George
Would halt his horse to rest after the pull,
Himself fill lungs with wine-like air from the moor,
And lift up voice in clear, quavering tenor,
With 'What is your One-o? One of Them
Is all alone and ever will remain so.'
(The parish is dedicated to the Trinity.)
The road runs downward now through china-clay
Villages with ancient rebarbative names:
Scredda, Rescorla, Hallaze and Stenalees,
A hog's spine of hill mounding the western sky,
Carluddon, Carloggas and Resugga Green,
Penwithick Stents and Treverbyn vean, a tree
Or two in a hollow by the cemetery.
The view to the right across prehistoric moors,
Full of crosses, quoits and standing stones,
Circles and monoliths and dead men's bones,
To Luxulyan tower suddenly lit by the sun.
Now for the indignity of nondescript
And very Methodist Carnsmerry: blow, Bugle, blow
Over the bitter cross-roads where through the thirties

I often spoke to a handful of lounging men
Of the approaching war, the wrath to come.
Some of them are dead. Here lives still one
Of the faithful, stalwart son now at college.
Enter the last lap, a shallow valley
Of settling-pools, clay-dries and small farms,
Tall chimneys punctuate the tilted slope
To where at the top the immense, frowning Rock
Of the medieval hermit looms and threatens,
Broken arch of chapel an eyehole at summit,
The eye of a needle the rich may not enter.
Here he kept vigil among the mad winds
Racing across the moor, swirling among rocks
Like up-ended sarcophagi awaiting the doom.
Here walled up, a local Stylites,
He lived on his winnard's perch, kept in food
By the flock in return for his offering of prayer,
Fulfilling the function of psychologist to the folk,
Shaping their fantasies into satisfying form.
And so by the church-tower where Wesley preached,
Though his disciple Sam Furley would never follow,
Take scrip and staff and no thought for the morrow.
Down the descent by cobwalled Rock Inn
To the sombre garden where my ancient friend awaits me,
Eyes blue as periwinkle in the border,
A rich and warm expressive Cornish voice,
With the crackle in it like foot on autumn leaves,
Smile like the early April sun coming out
Among windswept daffodils, their heads blown,
Spilled cups of gold upon clumps of heather
In this rockbound moorland fastness hemmed about
By all the temerarious flowers of spring.

Passion Sunday in Charlestown Church

The rain beats down remorselessly
From beech and chestnut on the graves;
My young cousin lies beside the porch.
The parish is all gathered in the church,
The minute bell clangs, last footsteps hurry,
The Mass about to begin.
The holy priest in blood-red chasuble
Brings in the elements, a lighted candle
Goes before; the handsome, dark-haired thurifer
Erect, a slimmer Felix Randal,
Comes down to cense the faithful.
He bows, the parish returns his salutation,
Even the one stray sheep (shall there not be joy in heaven
Over one sinner that repenteth,
More than over ninety and nine just persons?)
He has returned, unrepentant, not to pray,
But to watch, observe, mumble with his lips,
Go through the familiar childhood ritual,
Tears hardly held back from the eyes—
Hoping it might be so—while the chants rise:
    Kyrie Eleison,
    Christe Eleison,
    Kyrie Eleison.
Rain patters on the roof,
The wind rushes in the gutters,
Attention wanders, till the Creed:
And was incarnate by the Holy Ghost,
And was made man.
The parish falls on knees, then shuffles up again.
This is the Victorian church my father and mother
Were married in that Lenten day so long ago:
The simple courage, the confidence in life

Their son has never found, yet had beginning
In this place. Now come back,
A public man, scarred with injuries,
Seared by sad experience, without illusion
Or any hope, dedicated to despair.
What hope in these tender trumperies
That move the heart, but not the hardened mind?
The moment comes, thurifer and acolytes
Around the priest, aloft the lights,
The church all silent for the Consecration.
Tears burn behind the unbelieving eyes,
Knowing too well no miracle is here
But dear mnemonic mummery.
A hush falls, the sanctus bell clangs out over
My cousin's grave, eager and gallant youth,
Along the road he used to come to church,
Over the roofs and down to the harbour
Where Jim was drowned when I was a child—
They brought him home upon a poor man's cart.
At the Communion, one old sinner I used to know
In her more prosperous days returns to pew,
The haggard eyes not more suffused with tears
Than the known face that greets her after years
Looking up with a chaste and sad surprise.
The lights are out, the incense quenched,
The slim and stalwart thurifer
Back in his place in choir.
The moment of suspended time
Hung between now and eternity is over,
Tenderness floods into the ulcered heart
As the parish files out through the lych-gate
My parents entered some seventy years ago,
And scatters along the unrecoverable road.

Shoes

My shoes in the corner of the room,
Pair by pair in different attitudes:
In one I see myself going upstairs,
The right foot feeling for the lip,
The left already firmly planted on the step;
Two others lying apart, small boats
Tipped on their sides opposite each other,
Listlessly apart, as when sitting
Feet thrust out from comfortable arm-chair;
Another pair, heel to heel, slightly askew,
Others in order, prim and waiting two by two.
In all of them I see the stance of my mother,
At once affirmative and questioning,
Reluctant yet not afraid
To set out on her pilgrimage,
Now long arrived, the journey over.

Contingent Beauty

I do not wish to die—
There is such contingent beauty in life:
The open window on summer mornings
Looking on gardens and green things growing,
The shadowy cups of roses flowering to themselves
—Images of time and eternity—
Silence in the garden and felt along the walls.
The room is suddenly filled with sun,
Like a sacrament one can never be
Sufficiently thankful for. Door ajar,
The eye reaches across from one
Open window to another, eye to eye,
And then the healing spaces of the sky.
How can one think of life as evil,
The world as made by blackguard or brute
When so much beauty lies on every hand
Waiting only to reach out and touch the fruit,
The sensitive soul to wait upon
Moments of apprehension,
Of satisfaction inexpressible,
Penetration of the whole being
In the early morning silence and the sun
Before the day begins to stir?

The Faithful Unbeliever

I stand on the steps of St. Peter's, Eaton Square,
Sparrows chirping under the tall colonnade,
The flowering cherry all in surpliced white,
Daffodils and bluebells this late reluctant May:
Rain and sun and wind, the scent of flowers,
The mingled beauty and sadness of the spring.
Two boy-friends eat their office-lunch on the steps.
Within, here is the sanctuary where he served.
The verger says, 'He left before I came.
Several members of the congregation remember him.
He died this year, didn't he?'
This is where he served his first curacy,
A frisky young cleric straight from college,
Tall and boyish, full of pranks and fun.
Here's the pulpit where he preached his sermons
Beneath the hanging Master whom he served.
A secret stillness holds within this place,
Punctuated, not disturbed, by the traffic without.
Here's the font where he baptized, the scene
Of play-acting that was not all play-acting.
Spring flowers light up the sanctuary
With their gold. A flickering morning light
Passes over the altar where he often knelt,
Not at ease with himself, with difficulty
Attempting to follow in his Master's footsteps,
Not often achieving it, yet not wholly out.
Victorian mosaic and gilt, brass eagle and screen,
The angels look down upon the human scene:
Sunday by Sunday the choirboys and servers,
The rich dowagers of the Square, the streets around,
The School journey to his native Newquay,
The boys' Swimming Gala at St. George's Baths,

The multifarious errands of the parish,
The life of good works, not unscathed by sin.
'He that is without sin among you, let him first cast a stone.'
O, Anthony, how could it have come to this?
The fruitful life, the unsteady course, still
Yielding good, ended by its own will,
After what anguish of mind, what suffering,
Snuffed out like the sunlight flickering
On the altar, passing and repassing
This uncertain spring, perhaps a sign
Of recognition to one lingering in the church—
Darkness in the sanctuary as he withdraws—
The faithful unbeliever, remembering.

On the Sea Front at Hornsea: My Fifty-Fifth Birthday

Fifty four years have now flown over me:
I celebrate my birthday by the northern sea
At Hornsea, Marine View and Esplanade,
Houses and Properties for sale by Arthur Toby,
Pitch and Putt at 6d. per Round.
The summer beauties of both sexes have
Departed, leaving the seafront to the sun and me.
Nothing but the pitch and putt of the sea,
Nothing in view of Flamborough Head and Spurn
In the light sea-haze of early December.
Nothing but the faint indecipherable smell
Of lemon or thyme lost amid the tattered ragwort.
The strangulated cries of water-birds
Float over from Hornsea Mere. Nothing but
A puff of December breeze in my hair,
The imprint of the sun upon the page as I write.
The Ladies' Luncheon awaits the greying man,
The *commis voyageur* of culture,
In the Floral Hall. I have come through
The rich black loam of Holderness
Turned over, gleaming fishbacks in the sun.
The red-faced, sharp-nosed farmers drive
Occasionally by in black Rolls-Royces.
The immense fields gently undulate,
Waves of the sea from which they came,
The haystacks like cathedrals on the horizon.
Leaning over the seaward balustrade,
Amid thyme and ragwort, a sprig of rosemary:
The thought—'I have not twenty years to live'.

St. Anne's-on-the-Sea

In the late afternoon of my life I lie and doze
In the residents' lounge of the hotel at Lytham St. Anne's,
The candid sun full on my February face
White and drawn with long winter's overwork.
Behind me the silvery chime of a Victorian clock
Tinkles the afternoon tea-time hour away.
No-one about: no-one walks on the sands:
The sea-side resort is deserted, the turreted stands
Of the pier silent and empty as a cathedral.
The quietude of the sea-birds can be heard,
Made more still by one dreamy liquid whirr.
In tunnelled euonymus and veronica
A little cat plays a solitary game
Of hide and seek by herself, animal emblem
In the solipsistic human universe.
The sea's melancholy withdrawing roar
I hear far out from the paved, cemented shore,
Where an old rheumatic couple cripple along
To take their daily ration of regular air.
Above the remote and corrugated sands
A covey of oyster-catchers rise and fly
Decoratively along the edge of sea and sky:
A water-colour of Girtin or David Cox.
Nearer, the architecture of the Edwardian age,
Minarets and domes, endearing lampstands,
Along North Promenade and South, the Blackpool Road,
St. Ives' hotel, Glendower and the Esplanade.
Slowly the sun goes down behind the bank
Of low nimbus cloud over the grey waters.
The tide is on the turn and inward comes
Darkness and the ice-cold winter sea.

February Day in the Iffley Road

O February day of consequence and cloud,
High wind blowing ladies' hats off in the street,
Where television's calligraphy scrawls
Insignificance along the squalid roofs.
The copper hydrangeas rust in corners;
Here Mr. Wells does High Class Boot Repairs,
Or did in the early nineteen hundreds,
When the gas-lamp focussed the assignations
Of the street. Now all is in a state of disrepair,
Blinds, windows, gates fly open with the wind;
The Capuchin Greyfriars climb their greasy stair
To their lighthouse view of the world, over
Chester Street and Daubeny Street and where
Bedford Street bends round to fill-dyke marshes
Swept by the wind and across to woods of Wytham,
Where bluebells and cuckoo-pint grew
Before time was, when all the world was young.

In Place of Love

In place of love
One purchases deception by the hour
Wide-eyed and well aware—
After all, the assumption is not complimentary—
Waiting in hotel-bedrooms for a knock on the door,
Or at street-corners for a look from the eye,
Adventures on pavements that serve but to disabuse,
Ingenuously disingenuous, innocent
Yet full of intent,
By no means taken in:
Amused not at the other, but at oneself,
Inviting the laugh upon oneself,
Though not precisely welcoming it,
The familiar outcome,
The exchange of mutual insincerities,
Each knowing how to take the other's compliments,
The facile tongues, the easy flatteries—
Nothing moved, save another small corrosion of the heart,
Another indecipherable film of scar-tissue
Across the wounded place, whence comes no love,
Accepting all, not in place of love,
But chiefly for the sake of the poem.

The White Cat of Trenarren

(for Beryl Cloke)

He was a mighty hunter in his youth
At Polmear all day on the mound, on the pounce
For anything moving, rabbit or bird or mouse—
My cat and I grow old together.

After a day's hunting he'd come into the house
Delicate ears stuck all with fleas.
At Trenarren I've heard him sigh with pleasure
After a summer's day in the long-grown leas—
My cat and I grow old together.

When I was a child I played all day,
With only a little cat for companion,
At solitary games of my own invention
Under the table or up in the green bay—
My cat and I grow old together.

When I was a boy I wandered the roads
Up to the downs by gaunt Carn Grey,
Wrapt in a dream at end of day,
All round me the moor, below me the bay—
My cat and I grow old together.

Now we are too often apart, yet
Turning out of Central Park into the Plaza,
Or walking Michigan Avenue against the lake-wind,
I see a little white shade in the shrubbery
Of far-off Trenarren, never far from my mind—
My cat and I grow old together.

When I come home from too much travelling,
Cautiously he comes out of his lair to my call,

Receives me at first with a shy reproach
At long absence to him incomprehensible—
My cat and I grow old together.

Incapable of much or long resentment,
He scratches at my door to be let out
In early morning in the ash moonlight,
Or red dawn breaking through Mother Bond's spinney—
My cat and I grow old together.

No more frisking as of old,
Or chasing his shadow over the lawn,
But a dignified old person, tickling
His nose against twig or flower in the border,
Until evening falls and bed-time's in order,
Unable to keep eyes open any longer
He waits for me to carry him upstairs
To nestle all night snug at foot of bed—
My cat and I grow old together.

Careful of his licked and polished appearance,
Ears like shell-whorls pink and transparent,
White plume waving proudly over the paths,
Against a background of sea and blue hydrangeas—
My cat and I grow old together.

West Country Folksong: Child's Verses for Winter

Devon was white,
But Cornwall was green:
The prettiest sight
That ever was seen.

When Cornwall was copper
Devon was gold:
On moorland and hilltop,
Pasture and fold.

When Devon was purple
Cornwall was brown,
With harvesting bracken
On ledra and down.

When Cornwall was grey
With sea-mist and spume,
Devon was greenest
With apples in bloom.

Devon was shrouded
With snow on each thing,
But Cornwall was verdant
With promise of spring.